What You Didn't Learn in Sunday School

What You Didn't Learn in Sunday School

Women Who Didn't Shut Up and Sit Down

Shawna R. B. Atteberry

RESOURCE *Publications* · Eugene, Oregon

To my husband, Tracy Atteberry

The Lappidoth to my Deborah

Contents

Contents

Acknowledgments

FIRST I WOULD LIKE to thank my guinea pigs: the Thursday night Bible study group that meets at Chicago Grace Episcopal Church: Rector Ted Cutis, Andrea Barnhardt, Jacki Pingel-Biddy, Robert and Sharon Novickas, and Taylor Rockhill. I taught this material for a month to get a feel for what needed to go into this book. Your questions and insights helped me to see old and treasured stories in new ways, which have made this a better book.

I would also like to thank my readers who gave me valuable feedback, as well as let me interview them for the podcasts: Sandi Amorim, Catherine Caine, J. K. Gayle, Roxanne Krystalli, Mark Mattison, Lainie Petersen, and Jacki Pingel-Biddy. Thank you for taking the time to read the book and share your thoughts with me. A special thanks to Mark Mattison for writing the forward and reading through the book twice, making valuable insights about the content as well as catching many typos.

A special thanks to my husband, Tracy, who has encouraged me to pursue my dreams. He designed the original E-book I self-published. There is nothing better than being married to a person who supports you in what you believe you are called to do. I'm a very lucky woman.

A final and heartfelt thank you to all of you who have read my blog, bought the self-published version of this book, supported me, and prayed for me over the last six years. It's been quite a journey for me, with changes in my life that I could not even imagine in the beginning. I feel honored you have chosen to share the last few years with me.

Foreword

RARELY DOES ONE COME across a book so compelling that it's impossible to encounter it and remain unchanged. This book by the Rev. Shawna R.B. Atteberry is one of those rare gems. *What You Didn't Learn in Sunday School* is at once academically responsible and eminently accessible to a broad audience, making it an ideal resource for Bible studies.

Some of the biblical women described in this book are very familiar–women like Deborah and Priscilla, for example–but others are much less well known. Do you remember the daughters of Zelophehad, who dared to question Moses? What about the Wise Woman of Abel who negotiated with a military general? Regardless of how well-known these stories may be, however, each chapter provides new and penetrating insights guaranteed to help us stop and think about them in delightful new ways.

Part of the genius of Rev. Atteberry's approach–what enables some of us really to *see*, for the first time, what we never did see when we first learned some of these stories in Sunday School–is her consistent juxtaposition of so-called "complementarian" values (particularly silence and submission) with these remarkable narratives found liberally throughout both the Hebrew Scriptures and the New Testament. I've always known the story of

Abigail, for example, but much to my chagrin it never even occurred to me that her example clearly challenges the "complementarian" conviction that women should always submit to their husbands.

Reading these ancient stories through the lens of our contemporary debate about women's rights not only clarifies the issues, it broadens the foundation for a truly biblical position. It's not simply a matter of wrangling over a few Greek words in the New Testament, nor of adjudicating between "traditional Judeo-Christian values" and "modern feminism." Building her case on the actual stories of Scripture rather than a handful of verses, Rev. Atteberry demonstrates that it's actually traditional patriarchalism, not contemporary feminism, that stands in sharp contrast to the view of women often reflected in the Bible.

The issues don't stop there, however. Rev. Atteberry's treatment also problematizes the Fundamentalist view of Scripture as "inerrant" in every respect. This is vitally important because an uncompromising "inerrant" approach to Scripture necessarily flattens out the biblical witness into hopelessly irreconcilable texts, silencing some narratives in order to privilege a handful of other texts which clearly reflect the patriarchal values of ancient societies rather than the countercultural liberation of Godde's good news. Ironically, it's actually the Fundamentalist approach that finally distorts the biblical witness. Allowing each text to stand on its own, irrespective of the testimony of select "control texts," enables us more honestly to evaluate <u>all</u> of the evidence, not just the convenient, "cherry-picked" parts that happen to suit our preconceived stereotypes about gender and class.

Rev. Atteberry challenges those who privilege the "household codes" of the New Testament to admit the underlying cultural basis of those values: The conviction that women, children, and slaves were the "property" of men who were the respective "heads" of their households. She rightfully aligns the issue of women's status with that of slavery, poignantly arguing that what's true of the one must be true of the other. If Evangelicals candidly admit that the very idea of slavery–which ancient Jews and Christians tolerated (at best) and endorsed (at worst)– more accurately reflects primitive, imperial worldly values rather than the original intention of Godde, then they should also be willing to concede that the idea of women's subjugation is just as outmoded.

Finally, however, Rev. Atteberry takes her argument a step further, demonstrating in her own straightforward and lucid way that the two New Testament passages most often cited to suppress women are not nearly as clear-cut as we may think. Specifically, if the historical contexts of 1 Corinthians 14:33*b*-35 and 1 Timothy 2:11-15 afford more plausible interpretations, these texts may not have been originally intended to dictate an unchanging law for all churches in all places at all times. Though it's difficult to establish the meanings of these texts with absolute certainty, the very existence of multiple (plausible) interpretations should itself be enough to counsel humility, discouraging us from rushing to judgment "where angels fear to tread."

As you'll discover within these pages, Rev. Atteberry is an exemplary feminist scholar whose years of pastoral experience significantly enrich the many insights she has to share. In addition to her work as a writer, theologian, and storyteller, Rev. Atteberry is also an Associate

Editor of the *Divine Feminine Version* (DFV) of the New Testament, which she uses in this current manuscript. I'm privileged to know her not only as a colleague and personal friend, but as a spiritual mentor as well.

Mark M. Mattison
Co-General Editor, the *Divine Feminine Version* (DFV)
of the New Testament

Introduction

To HEAR SOME PEOPLE talk, you'd think that the Bible was full of stories, chapters, and verses declaring that women should have no authority anywhere. Women should always be in submission to a man whether it be father, husband, or church leader. They can't be trusted to teach, preach, or lead because that is the way they were made. Not to mention Eve was the first one to sin, so that means women must be more gullible and easily deceived than men.

Those who believe women are to be submissive and under the authority of men in all aspects of life are known as "complementarians." But here's the thing: the complementarians are wrong. The Bible is not chock full of stories about female submission to the all-mighty male. In fact, only eight verses out of over 30,000 verses in the Bible talk about female submission and silence. Just eight verses. These eight verses are used as a prism to interpret every other story, chapter, and verse in the Bible regarding women. If the story or passage does not line up with these eight verses, then it must be properly explained as to what Godde really meant. The chapters and stories that do show women in leadership roles in the home, community and spiritually are explained away, neglected and ignored. If these women have to be mentioned then their authority and power are marginalized, and the story is often retold casting the strong woman as a good, submissive wife. These are the women you don't learn about in Sunday School. Or if you do learn about them, they are altered beyond recognition from the Biblical witness.

Those eight little verses

What are these eight little verses that control how women through thousands of years of Jewish and Christian history are portrayed? What are these eight little verses that are used to keep women in their proper silent and submissive place in both The Hebrew Scriptures and the New Testament? Here they are:

> Women should keep quiet in the communities, because they aren't allowed to speak; but they should be submissive, as the Torah says. If they want to learn anything, they should ask their own husbands at home, because it's shameful for a woman to speak in the community.
> What? Did the message of Godde originate with you? Or are you the only ones it reached? (1 Corinthians 14:33-35).

> There is a woman who needs to quietly receive instruction in submission. I don't want her to teach or to upstage her husband, but to keep quiet, because Adam was formed first, then Eve; and Adam wasn't tricked, but Eve was tricked and became a lawbreaker; and women who have children will be given life, provided they continue in trust, love, and holiness with self-restraint (1 Timothy 2:11-15).

If you just went "Huh?" don't worry, you're not the only one. It's shameful for a woman to speak in church? A woman has to keep silent because of Eve? And my personal favorite: Women "will be given life [saved] through childbearing." (This is my favorite because my husband and I have chosen not to have children. Am I unsaveable?)

So, what are we in the 21st century supposed to think about this? Do Christians (particularly Christian women) have to be held in rigid gender roles based on these verses? Do women have no choice but to sit down and shut up because these eight verses are used to marginalize and negate every Scripture regarding women working, women making their own decisions, and women in authority? That's the way these eight verses have been used through the 2,000 years of the Christian Church. But I've learned that just because something in the Bible has been interpreted in a certain way for millennia doesn't mean that interpretation is right. Look at slavery. Over 100 years ago American Christians were using passages in the Bible to justify slavery. Now no American is going to use those passages in Scripture to justify slavery today. We recognize that even though it's endorsed in the Bible, slavery is wrong. It's unethical. We've changed how we interpret the slavery passages in the Bible. Why can't we change how we interpret the passages about women?

According to those who want to interpret the Bible literally as the inerrant word of Godde in all things, to do this would be to undermine all of Christianity. But all of Christianity wasn't undermined by not literally obeying the passages about slavery. Why are women so different? My answer is: it's no different. In fact, my challenge to the inerrantists is to take their literalism to its logical conclusion. In the Near Eastern world that is the setting of the Bible, women were property. That's why instructions to women, children, and slaves were lumped together: they were all the property of the man who was the head of the household, or the *paterfamilias*. We now believe it is not right for one human being to own another: slavery is illegal. We no longer believe that children are the property of their parents; in fact, children are taken away from parents who neglect and abuse them. In First World countries (like the United States), we no longer believe that women are the property of men. The only way these verses make sense is if you continue to believe that women are the property of men. Women could not have authority over their husbands because they were property. Women had to submit to their husbands because they were property. So why do complementarians continue to take these verses literally when the foundation for these verses is no longer valid? I honestly don't know. They try to make it sound like they don't want to regard women as property. They contort the creation narratives in Genesis into all sorts of horrible shapes to show female submission is the way Godde meant things to be. But in the end, the only reason I can see that they hold so tenaciously to these verses is that they believe women are property.

They also don't admit that there are major translation issues with these verses, and both epistles these verses show up in were written to very troubled churches about very specific situations. They do not want to admit these verses are not as cut and dry as they seem, and they refuse to admit that these instructions were just for that place for that time (like slavery). They want to make these verses universal, meant for all time.

In the following chapters I will introduce you to the women in the Bible who will show us that these verses were never meant to be taken for all time, forever, amen. I've divided them into three groups: women who didn't submit, women who didn't shut up, and women who held authority over both men and women, mainly as religious leaders. We will see that women through the course of biblical history may have been viewed as the property of men, but they didn't act like it. They stood their ground, they spoke their minds, they made decisions that changed the course of Godde's people, and they were leaders in both secular and sacred circles.

In the last two chapters we'll look at the verses we read about from 1 Corinthians and 1 Timothy, the "problem verses," as they are called. I'm going to describe the historical and sociological background to these letters. Then I'm going to show the different ways these verses can be translated. Finally, I'll show there are interpretations of these verses that are true to the Bible as sacred scripture but do not shackle women as the property of men.

The Appendix will help you get started, or continue, your own study of these incredible women, and there is a Recommended Reading list to help you choose Bible dictionaries, commentaries, and other resources that will help you understand the historical and sociological background of the Bible, and the world these fabulous women lived in.

A few explanations and definitions

Before we go any further, here are the definitions of some words you'll see throughout this study.

Godde: This is the word I use in place of God. "Godde" is a combination of the words "God" and "Goddess." It's intended to show that Godde is both male and female and transcends both genders. If we believe Genesis 1:27, which says Godde made both male and female in Godde's image, then we have to seriously look at the metaphors and language we use for Godde to make sure Godde is imaged as both male and female, to show both sexes are needed to fully image Godde on earth.

I've used the *Divine Feminine Version* for the New Testament for this reason: it uses Godde in place of God and feminine pronouns for Godde, so there is a balance of masculine and feminine in the Scripture passages. I should add a disclaimer: I'm one of the associate editors working to translate the New Testament for The Divine Feminine translation project.

Yahweh: This is the name for Godde in the Hebrew Scriptures, YHWH. We are not sure how it is pronounced because the Jewish people never speak the Holy Name. In English translations of the Bible it is translated as LORD. I've chosen to use the World English Bible for the passages from the Old Testament because this translation uses Yahweh instead of LORD. I've made adaptations to this public domain Bible to make it gender inclusive of both Godde and people.

Evangelical: The Evangelical movement in the United States believes that a person has to make a personal profession of faith in Jesus Christ or be "born again." They believe that Jesus is the only way to Godde and heaven, and they are called to save people—convince them to enter a personal relationship with Jesus. Being born again often includes saying a prayer in which the person confesses to being a sinner, repenting (promising not to live their old life anymore), and declares that Jesus is their Savior and the only way to Godde. The confession of faith is normally followed by baptism. The Evangelical movement in the United States has gone through major shifts in its short history. In the late 19th and early 20th centuries, Evangelicals were on the forefront of the social justice movement in the United States. They were the ones who opened homes for unwed mothers and orphanages; they rehabilitated alcoholics and drug addicts, helped them find work and get homes; and they were involved in the fight for women's right to vote and better working conditions in factories and workplaces. Evangelical women fought for a fair wage, limiting how many hours workers could work a week, and laws against sexual harassment. After World War II this group became insular and created a Christian sub-culture where they would be safe from worldly influences. In the 1980s the movement morphed once again into the political arena where their hallmark became fighting against abortion and equal rights for gays, as well as gay marriage. These became known as "the culture wars." Currently, evangelicalism is undergoing another shift. Younger evangelicals (under 35 years old) are leaving the culture war mentality and want to embrace a larger and more historical Christianity. They are concerned about working conditions of people around the world making a fair wage, oppressive power structures, the environment, and promoting peace. Through all of these changes the one thing that has remained a constant in the Evangelical movement is its exclusivist belief that salvation comes only through Jesus by being born again, which means they do not see infant baptism and confirmation as proof that one is Christian. Nor do they see a continual walk towards Godde as "salvation." There has to be that born again experience, one moment you can point to and say, "That's when I was saved. That's when my relationship with Godde began."

Fundamentalism: In this book "fundamentalism" refers to a group within Evangelical Christianity that believes the Bible is the inerrant word of God in all things pertaining to life: history, science, salvation, and how we should live. These are the people who believe Godde literally created the world in seven days, and if the Bible alludes to history and science then that's how it had to happen. They think Godde literally dictated Scripture to those who wrote the Bible, and therefore it is the inerrant word of Godde. They think the same social structures Godde worked through in biblical times gave those structures divine mandate. They believe that Godde created patriarchy as the biblical and godly way to live. They believe that because Godde created the woman second in one of the creation accounts (Genesis 2), this means she is to be submissive to her husband in all things: always obeying him, and never questioning his authority because it is his Godde-given role to be the head of the house and its spiritual priest. He is responsible for his family living holy and godly lives. They also tend to believe a couple should accept as many children as Godde gives, and birth control should not be used. A woman's role is in the home, being a wife and mother. That is her Godde-given assignment in life. They take the verses in 1 Corinthians and 1 Timothy literally in both the church and home. Women are always to be quiet and submissive, not having authority over men in any realm of life.

Part 1

Women Who Didn't Shut Up

Chapter 1

The Daughters of Zelophehad

Then the daughters of Zelophehad, the son of Hepher, the son of Gilead, the son of Machir, the son of Manasseh, of the families of Manasseh the son of Joseph came forward. These are the names of his daughters: Mahlah, Noah, Hoglah, Milcah, and Tirzah. They stood at the door of the Tent of Meeting before Moses, Eleazar the priest, the leaders, and all the people, saying, "Our father died in the wilderness. He was not among the company of those who gathered together against Yahweh in the company of Korah, but he died in his own sin. He had no sons. Why should our father's name be taken away from among his family, because he had no son? Give us a possession among the brothers of our father."

Moses brought their cause before Yahweh. Yahweh spoke to Moses, saying, "Zelophehad's daughters are right in what they say. You will give them a possession of an inheritance among their father's brothers. You will give their father's inheritance to them. You will speak to the children of Israel and say, 'If a man dies, and has no son, then you will give his inheritance to his daughter. If he has no daughter, then you shall give his inheritance to his brothers. If he has no brothers, then you shall give his inheritance to

> his father's brothers. If his father has no brothers,
> then you shall give his inheritance to the closest
> relative in his family, and he shall possess it. This
> shall be a statute and ordinance for the children
> of Israel, as Yahweh commanded Moses.'"
> —Numbers 27:1–11

In Numbers 26, land was apportioned out to the twelve tribes of Israel. After taking control of the land east of the Jordan, the Israelites were preparing to cross over the Jordan River to the western lands promised to their ancestors: Abraham and Sarah, Isaac and Rebekah, and Jacob, Leah, and Rachel. After taking a census, land was apportioned out to each clan and family. There was only one problem: only men could inherit land. The five daughters of Zelophehad had a problem with this. If only men inherited land, their father's name and legacy would be lost. Mahlah, Noah, Hoglah, Milcah, and Tirzah did not sit idly by and blindly submit to the law (or Moses). They took their case to Moses. Since they had no brothers, they wished to inherit their father's land, so Zelophehad's name would remain in the tribe and Israel.

Moses did not have a ready answer for this, so he brought the sisters' case to Yahweh. This is only one of four times in the Torah a legal situation calls for special revelation. Godde agreed with the sisters, and told Moses: "Zelophehad's daughters are right in what they say. You will give them a possession of an inheritance among their father's brothers" (Numbers 27:7). They would be place holders until they married and had children. Their sons would inherit the land.

1. What do the actions of Mahlah, Tirzah, Hoglah, Milcah, and Noah tell us about these sisters?

2. What do the sister's actions say about how they see Godde?

The heads of the households of the children of Gilead, the son of Machir, the son of Manasseh, of the families of the sons of Joseph came forward and spoke to Moses, the leaders, and the heads of the households of the children of Israel. They said, "Yahweh commanded my lord to give the land for inheritance by lot to the children of Israel. My lord was commanded by Yahweh to give the inheritance of Zelophehad our brother to his daughters. If they marry men from other tribes of Israel then their inheritance will be taken away from the inheritance given to our ancestors, and will be added to the land of the tribe they marry into. It will be taken away from our inheritance. When the jubilee of the children of Israel happens, their inheritance will be added to the inheritance of the tribe they married into. So their inheritance will be taken away from the inheritance of our ancestor's tribe."

Moses commanded the children of Israel according to Yahweh's word, saying, "The tribe of Joseph speaks correctly. Here is what Yahweh commands concerning Zelophehad's daughters, 'Let them be married to whom they think best; only they shall marry into the family of their father's tribe. This way no inheritance of the children of Israel will move from tribe to tribe. The children of Israel shall all keep the inheritance of their ancestors' tribes. Every daughter who possesses an inheritance in any of Israel's tribes will marry a man from her father's tribe that the children of Israel may each possess the inheritance of their ancestors, so no inheritance will move from one tribe to another tribe. The tribes of the children of Israel shall keep their own inheritance.'"
—Numbers 36:1–9

In Numbers 36 we encounter the five sisters again. This time the men of the tribe are afraid of losing part of their land if the sisters marry outside of the tribe. In the Bible a woman always went to live with her husband's family, which meant her husband's family would gain control of the inherited land, and the tribe of Manasseh might lose land given to it to another tribe. This time Moses did not consult Godde; he gave a ruling. He acknowledged the men of the tribe were right, and commanded the daughters of Zelophehad to marry within the tribe of Manasseh, so that the land would stay within their tribe. The sisters obeyed and married men of their tribe. I'm guessing at least one of their sons was named Zelophehad. The final passage in Joshua shows that Joshua fulfilled the oath given to the five daughters. After Israel took control of the land, Mahlah, Tirzah, Hoglah, Milcah, and Noah inherited their father's land, and his name or legacy was not forgotten.

Chapter 2

The Wise Woman of Abel

There happened to be a scoundrel whose name was Sheba, the son of Bichri, a Benjamite. He blew the trumpet and said, "We have no portion in David, neither have we inheritance in the son of Jesse. Everyone to their tents, Israel!" So all the people of Israel stopped following David and followed Sheba the son of Bichri. But the people of Judah joined with their king, from the Jordan even to Jerusalem.
—2 Samuel 20:1–2

Sheba passed through all the tribes of Israel to Abel of Beth Maacah with all the Berites. They were gathered together in the city. Joab and his forces came and besieged them in Abel of Beth Maacah, and they built siege ramps against the city. All the people who were with Joab battered the wall, to throw it down. Then a wise woman cried out of the city, "Listen, listen! Please say to Joab, 'Come near here, that I may speak with you.'" He came near to her, and the woman said, "Are you Joab?"

He answered, "I am."

Then she said to him, "Listen to the words of your servant."

He answered, "I'm listening."

> Then she spoke, "They used to say in old times, 'Let them ask counsel at Abel,' and so they settled a matter. I am among those who are peaceful and faithful in Israel. You seek to destroy a city and a mother in Israel. Why will you swallow up Yahweh's inheritance?"
>
> Joab answered, "Far be it from me, far be it, that I should swallow up or destroy. This is not the case. But a man of the hill country of Ephraim, Sheba the son of Bichri by name, has lifted up his hand against the king, against David. Just deliver him, and I will depart from the city."
>
> The woman said to Joab, "His head will be thrown to you over the wall."
>
> Then the woman went to all the people in her wisdom. They cut off the head of Sheba the son of Bichri, and threw it out to Joab. He blew the trumpet, and they left the city, everyone to their tents. Then Joab returned to Jerusalem to the king.
>
> —2 Samuel 20:14–22

After instigating a rebellion against King David, the traitor Sheba fled to Abel. David's general, Joab, followed Sheba and besieged the city. A Wise Woman of the town called out to Joab and wanted to know why Joab was attacking her city.

1. Do you find it odd that a woman is the one who asks a general why he's attacking her city?

2. Does Joab act like it is odd for this woman to be representing her city and apparently is one of its leaders?

When the Wise Woman called Joab to the wall for parlay, Joab treated her as an equal. We should note it didn't faze him that he was negotiating with a woman. He didn't act like this was unusual. This Wise Woman held political power in this town, and it didn't seem out of the ordinary, which tells us being wise didn't just mean she was smart: Wise Woman was a leadership and political position like that of town elder.[1]

The Wise Woman wanted to know why Joab was attacking a city who was "a mother in Israel." We learn from this woman Abel was a city known for its wisdom in settling matters between conflicting parties. There are only two places in the Bible where the "mother in Israel" metaphor is used. One is here in 2 Samuel 20:19 describing the city of Abel of Beth-maacah, and the other is in Judges 5:7 where Deborah is called a mother in Israel. In both of these instances a woman is a leader who saves her people. What does "mother of Israel" mean? I think the woman goes on to explain the metaphor: in the past it was said, "Let them ask counsel at Abel" (2 Sam. 20:18). Abel was renown for its ability to resolve conflicts. Just as people came to Moses, Samuel, and Deborah to help them resolve their conflicts, they came to Abel for their differences to be reconciled and peace restored. It was a peace-making city, faithful in Israel–a description which the woman may have intended to emphasize its support of David–which happened to have a traitor within its walls.

The Wise Woman also told Joab that Abel was "Yahweh's inheritance" (v. 19). Earlier in 1 Samuel when the mother of Tekoa (another Wise Woman) pled her case to David, she called her son "the inheritance of Godde" (2 Sam 14:16). In the previous chapter we saw the inheritance of land was referred to as Yahweh's inheritance. Yahweh's inheritance was something Yahweh gave

1. See Tikva Frymer-Kensky, *Reading the Women of the Bible*, "A Wise Woman of Power," 58–63.

to the people whether children or land. This inheritance was viewed as worth fighting for. "A mother in Israel" was a city or person who was renown for their wisdom and negotiating skills. They were able to bring about resolutions, protecting the inheritance of Yahweh from those who would destroy it.

We see the power this Wise Woman had in her city when she told Joab, "His head will be thrown to you over the wall." In the Hebrew she speaks as if it is already done: "Look! His head is thrown to you over the wall."[2] She had enough authority in the city that she didn't tell Joab she would go talk to the people; she told Joab it would be done. And it was: the people listened to her, killed Sheba, and threw his head to Joab.

The Wise Woman herself was "a mother in Israel." She showed all of the characteristics of her city: she had wisdom and negotiating skills, and she was a leader. She wanted to protect her city, which was the heritage of Yahweh. She had a man killed in order to secure the well-being of her city. This woman was the elder, and in all likelihood, the military commander of Abel, and that was why Joab negotiated with her: she was his equal.

1. Why does Joab negotiate with the Wise Woman if women are not supposed to have authority over men (the Wise Woman had authority over the men in the city)?

2. If this woman would have kept her mouth shut, what would have happened to her city?

---

2. Frymer-Kensky, *Reading the Women of the Bible*, 61.

Chapter 3

The Syro-Phoenician Woman

One Story, Two Gospels,
Two Interpretations

Mark's Story

Jesus left that place and went to the region of Tyre. He went into a house and didn't want anyone to know it, but he couldn't escape notice. A woman whose little daughter had a corrupting spirit heard about him and immediately came and fell down at his feet. She was a Greek, born in Syrian Phoenicia. She begged him to cast the demon out of her daughter. Jesus said to her, "Let the children eat first, because it's not right to throw the children's bread to the dogs."

"Lord," she replied, "even the dogs under the table eat the children's crumbs."

He said, "For saying that, you may go. The demon has left your daughter."

She went home and found the child lying on the bed. The demon was gone.

—Mark 7:24–30

We don't hear much about women giving Jesus lip in our churches. In the biblical witness we find two women who talked back to Jesus: Martha, the sister of Mary and Lazarus, and the Syro-Phoenician Woman in this passage. That these two women stood up to Jesus and talked back is usually explained away. In one scene, Martha was tired from cooking; in the other, her brother had just died: of course she's snippy, and Jesus is patient. In this scene, the Gentile woman knows that Jesus is just teasing her, and she plays along.

1. Do you think Jesus is teasing this woman? How would you know? How would she know?

2. Does the woman's response sound like she is being teased?

Martha and this woman's backbones are covered up, their nerve shoved into a corner. Neither of these women thought silence and submission was the way to go.

1. Skim through the first six chapters of Mark. What has Jesus been doing up until this point?

2. What is different about Jesus at the beginning of this story?

3. Do you think this is business as usual?

Jesus had been healing and teaching. He fed the multitude of 5,000. He had been debating (fighting) with the religious leaders. He came to a totally pagan, Gentile area to get away from everything. He was here for a break. He was not here to teach, to heal, or to fight. No one knew him here. He could sneak in, get some rest, and sneak out again. Or so he thought. Since Jesus was trying to stay incognito, we don't know how the woman knew he was in the neighborhood. My guess is through the local grapevine. She found out a great healer was in town, and she decided to act. If she had a husband, he's not mentioned. This mother acted on her own. She went to the house where Jesus was keeping a low profile, and there she fell at his feet begging him to heal her daughter, who was demon-possessed.

We expect Jesus to act immediately. We expect him to get up and go with this woman to her daughter, like he did with Jairus in the previous chapter. We also know from chapter 5 Jesus had no qualms about healing Gentiles: he healed the Gentile demoniac in the country of the Gerasenes. His first healing in Mark was healing a man with leprosy by touching him. But what we expect does not happen in this story.

Instead he told the woman, "It's not right to throw the children's bread to the dogs." At this point (if we are honest with ourselves) our jaws drop, and we wonder "What happened to Jesus?"

1. What do you think of this Jesus?
2. Is Jesus just tired and wanting to hide enough of an excuse to treat this woman the way he treated her?

A dog. Jesus called her a dog, a term of derision for Gentiles. They were unclean just as dogs were unclean. But pigs were unclean too, as well as graveyards, and Jesus did not call the Gerasenes demoniac a dog or swine. Why this abrupt change in Jesus? Does exhaustion alone account for it?

But the woman is quick-witted. She let the insult slide over her with this incisive retort: "Yes, but even the dogs get to lick up the crumbs on the floor." Fine. If he called her a dog then a dog she would be. She accepted what dogs accept: table scraps, crumbs, whatever those at the table deem worthy enough or inconsequential enough to give.

Because this woman did not shut up (or submit to the Son of Godde), because she stood her ground, Jesus changed his mind. He had not come here to heal. He didn't want to heal this woman's daughter. But in the end he did heal the daughter. He did because of the woman's retort. This woman's daughter was healed because she talked back to Jesus, and didn't assume her place was one of quiet submission.

1. Does your prayer life ever resemble this conversation?

2. Have you ever talked back to Godde? How do you feel about talking to Godde as this woman talked to Jesus?

3. How would this idea affect your own prayer life?

Matthew's Story

Jesus left that place and went to the region of Tyre and Sidon. A Canaanite woman came out, "Have mercy on me, Lord, son of Bathsheba and David!" she cried. "My daughter is severely oppressed by a demon!"

But he didn't say a thing.

His disciples came and begged him, "Send her away," they said, "because she bothers us."

He answered, "I wasn't sent to anyone but the lost sheep of Israel."

But she approached and bowed to him, "Lord, help me," she said.

"It is not right to throw the children's bread to the dogs," he said.

"Yes, Lord," she said, "but even the dogs eat the crumbs that fall from their masters' table."

Then Jesus answered, "Woman, your trust is great! What you want will be done for you." Her daughter was healed that very hour.
—Matthew 15:21–28

1. Compare Matthew's story to Mark's. What differences do you see?

2. How does the woman act in this story compared to Mark? What differences do you notice about her behavior?

3. What's different about the disciples?

4. Does Jesus act differently in this story?

5. What do you make of the differences? Do you think this story could be interpreted differently than Mark's story?

I'm sure you've figured out that this version of the story is going to be interpreted a little differently than Mark's version. This is another reason it's hard to say this is what Godde meant one time and forever more. The writers of the Bible gave different versions of stories with their own interpretations and application for their own communities. In Mark's version the disciples are invisible; in fact, they're not even mentioned. But not in Matthew; here they are front and center. I always figured it's because Matthew was uncomfortable with the Jesus in Mark being abrupt and rude (Matthew and Luke "fix" Mark quite a bit). But an Anglican priest I met in 2009 gave me another way to interpret this story.

Reverend Nadim Nassar grew up in Syria and went to school in Lebanon. He now lives in London. There is a very cultural thing he grew up with that explains perfectly what is going on in Matthew if we know Middle Eastern culture. In the Middle East when the eldest son marries, he still lives at home with his parents, and his wife comes to live with the family. This is because as the main heir, the eldest son is expected to take care of his parents in their old age.

When the mother-in-law doesn't like something the daughter-in-law is doing, or doesn't think the daughter-in-law is treating her with enough respect, the mother-in-law does not tell the daughter-in-law. She complains about it to a neighbor in the daughter's-in-law hearing.

"Miriam, do you know how my daughter-in-law treats me? I tell her every night, dry the dishes with a towel, don't air dry them! But does she listen to me?"

"Abraham, have I told you how my daughter-in-law doesn't respect me? I told her to water the garden this morning. Bah! Just look at my poor tomatoes withering away in this harsh sunlight!"

You get the idea. Now take this idea and apply it to the story. Jesus is the mother-in-law. The disciples are the daughters-in-law. The Canaanite woman is the neighbor. So what does that mean Jesus is doing in this story? In Mark's story Jesus is the one who's being exclusive, showing the members of Mark's community that even Jesus was corrected when he thought the gospel was just for the Jews. In Matthew, the disciples want Jesus to send the woman away, and he takes a minute to teach the disciples (Matthew's community) the gospel was not just for the Jews.

Jesus: "Look at my daughters-in-law thinking Godde is just for them. You called me 'Son of Bathsheba and David.' You know I can't take the kids' food and feed it to the dogs who come wandering in."

Woman: "Oh you poor thing. Such disrespect. But you know even the dogs get the crumbs the children leave behind."

Jesus (chuckling): "Woman you have great faith. Go. Your daughter is healed."

Woman looking at disciples' shocked faces: "Good luck with those daughters-in-law."

I said in Mark's story we could not read any humor or twinkling of eyes into that account. The only reason we can do that in this account is because of the disciples and what we know of Middle Eastern culture. This interpretation will not work in Mark because the disciples are not mentioned in the story. If they are in the room, they are silent. The scene is strictly between Jesus and the woman. And yes, Mark's account makes Jesus look bad, which is why Matthew added the disciples. They can look bad while Jesus appears to be an exasperated mother-in-law, which every woman who heard this story would understand. After all, they were all mothers-in-law or daughters-in-law: they lived out this situation every day.

1. What do you think of the differences in the accounts between Mark and Matthew?

2. Do you want to harmonize the two accounts and read Matthew into Mark, so Jesus doesn't look so surly?

3. Can you take each account on its own terms and live with the tension?

Part 2

Women Who Didn't Submit

Chapter 4

Tamar

It happened at about that time that Judah left his brothers, to go down and settle with a certain Adullamite called Hirah. There Judah saw the daughter of a Canaanite called Shua. He made her his wife and slept with her. She conceived and gave birth to a son whom she named Er. She conceived again and gave birth to a son whom she named Onan. Yet again she gave birth to a son whom she named Shelah. She was at Chezib when she gave birth to him. Judah took a wife for his first-born Er; her name was Tamar. But Er, Judah's first-born, offended Yahweh, and Yahweh killed him. Then Judah said to Onan, "Take your brother's wife, and do your duty as her brother-in-law, to maintain your brother's line." But Onan, knowing that the offspring would not be his, ejaculated on the ground every time he slept with his brother's wife, to avoid providing offspring for his brother. What he did was offensive to Yahweh who killed him too. Then Judah said to his daughter-in-law Tamar, "Go home as a widow to your father, until my son Shelah grows up," for he was thinking, "He must not die like his brothers." So Tamar went home to her father.

A long time passed, and then Shua's daughter, the wife of Judah, died. After Judah had been comforted he went up to Timnah for the shearing of his sheep with his friend Hirah the Adullamite. When Tamar was told, "Look, your father-in-law is going up to Timnah for the shearing of his sheep," she changed out of her widow's clothes, wrapped a veil around her to disguise herself, and sat down at the entrance to Enaim, which is on the way to Timnah. For she saw that, although Shelah was grown up, she had not been given to him as his wife. Judah saw her and took her for a prostitute, since her face was veiled. Going up to her on the road, he said, "Let me sleep with you." He did not know that she was his daughter-in-law.

"What will you give me for sleeping with you?" she asked.

"I will send you a kid from the flock," he said.

"Agreed, if you give me a pledge until you send it," she replied.

"What pledge shall I give you?" he asked.

"Your seal and cord and the staff you are holding," she replied. He gave them to her and slept with her, and she conceived by him. Then she got up and left him. Taking off her veil, she put back on her widow's clothing. Judah sent the kid by his friend the Adullamite to recover his pledge from the woman. But he did not find her. He inquired from the men of the place, "Where is the prostitute who was by the roadside at Enaim?"

"There is no prostitute there," they answered.

So returning to Judah he said, "I did not find her. What is more, the men of the place told me there had been no prostitute there." "Let her keep the things," Judah said, "or we shall become a laughing-stock. At least I sent her this kid, even though you did not find her."

About three months later, Judah was told, "Your daughter-in-law has played the whore; furthermore, she is pregnant, as a result of her misconduct."

"Bring her out," Judah ordered, "and let her be burnt alive!" But as she was being led off, she sent word to her father-in-law: "It was the owner of these who made me pregnant," she said. "Tell me whose seal, cord and staff these are."
Judah recognized them and said, "She was right and I was wrong, since I did not give her to my son Shelah."

He had no further intercourse with her. When the time came for her to give birth, there were twins in her womb! During the delivery, one of them put out a hand, and the midwife caught it and tied a scarlet thread to it, to show he was first born. Then he drew back his hand, and his brother was born. She said, "What a breach you have opened for yourself!" So he was named Perez. Then his brother was born with the scarlet thread on his hand, so he was named Zerah.
—Genesis 38:1–30

I know what you're thinking. What the heck is going on here? What kind of story is this? And it's in the Bible? Yes, this story is in the Bible, and it illustrates what was known as Levirate marriage. Remember the story of the daughters of Zelophehad we studied in the first section? They didn't want their father's name to die out because he had no sons, and therefore would not be given land. Levirate marriage was also concerned with a man's name not dying out, and the family land being lost. If a man died without children, his brother married his widow, and the first son born from the union would be considered the dead brother's son, and that son would inherit both his father's name and land. If there was no brother, the closest male relative married the widow.

This custom also protected the widow. Women who did not have a man and family's protection—whether father, husband or son—were put in a precarious position. They did not have a protector to care for them and defend them. If their former husband's family did not care for them, they could become beggars and prostitutes just to survive. By the brother marrying the widow then making sure she had a son, he insured her value in the family and gave her someone to care for her when she was old. This is the custom that underlies this story.

Tamar was first married to Judah's eldest son, Er, who did something Yahweh did not like and died. Judah commanded his second-born, Onan, to do his Levirate duty, to insure Er's lineage and provide economic support for Tamar. But Onan did not want to perpetuate Er's line. Onan's inheritance would be larger if Er did not have sons, so he performed *coitus interuptus* when he was having sex with Tamar so she would not get pregnant. This did not go over well with Yahweh, and Onan died for his disobedience.

Judah had a third son: Shelah. But now Judah was having second thoughts about giving another one of his sons to Tamar. It doesn't seem to matter that his sons' deaths were due to their sins and actions; Tamar must be a jinx. He sent her back to her father's house with the promise of marrying Shelah when he was older. Tamar obeyed and returned to her father's house, probably in disgrace as a childless widow.

- What do you think of the custom of Levirate marriage?
- How do you think Tamar felt about the situation she was put in?

- What are your feelings about Judah? Do you think he should have done more for Tamar?

Tamar initially obeyed and submitted to Judah. He was the patriarch, and therefore the head of the extended family. His word was law. Time passed and Judah's wife died. Tamar noticed Shelah was grown up, yet Judah had not called for her and given her to Shelah. Tamar decided not to submit anymore.

Reread what Tamar does.

- Does the story make any moral judgments about what Tamar does?

- What do Tamar's actions tell you about her?

- What do Judah's actions tell you about him?

Tamar decided she was not going to be sentenced to life as a childless widow. She devised a plan to make Judah keep his promise of a child. Remember the Levirate marriage did not have to be with a brother, but a close male relative. When told that Judah was going to a nearby town to shear his sheep, Tamar removed her widow's weeds, wrapped herself in a veil signifying she was a prostitute, and stationed herself at a crossroads. How did she know Judah would take advantage of a prostitute's services? Makes you wonder. Everything went according to plan, and she made sure she had proof of whom she slept with. In the next few verses we find out why it was so important to get Judah's signet, cord, and staff (his driver's license and credit card).

Three months later, Judah was told Tamar was pregnant. Considering the man just slept with a woman he thought was a prostitute, his reaction was brutal: "Bring her out . . . and let her be burnt alive!" (Gen 38:24). The double standard was in full swing. Tamar brought shame on the family by getting pregnant without the patriarch's permission, and now she would pay.

Tamar used her trump card. She sent the signet, cord, and staff to Judah with the message that the father of her child was the owner. Judah immediately recognized his belongings and admitted Tamar was right: "She is more righteous than I, inasmuch as I did not give her to my son Shelah" (v. 26, NASB). Judah admitted he did not keep his obligation to make sure his oldest son Er had heirs, and Tamar had the economic security that came with a son. He admitted she did the right thing, which made her more righteous than him.

Judah said Tamar was more righteous than him. The storyteller does not condemn Tamar or make any moral judgments regarding her action.

What do Tamar's actions show us about Godde?

Tamar goes on to bear twin sons, one of whom will be the ancestor of both King David and Jesus Christ. In Matthew's Gospel, Tamar will be one of four women named in Jesus' genealogy. Because Tamar was not willing to submit to Judah's will, she will always be remembered as one of the foremothers of Christ.

Chapter 5

Abigail

There was a man in Maon, whose possessions were in Carmel, and the man was very rich. He had three thousand sheep and a thousand goats, and he was shearing his sheep in Carmel. Now the name of the man was Nabal, and the name of his wife, Abigail. This woman was intelligent and had a beautiful face, but the man, a Calebite, was surly and evil in his doings. David heard in the wilderness that Nabal was shearing his sheep. David sent ten young men, saying to them, "Go up to Carmel, and go to Nabal, and greet him in my name. Tell him, 'Long life to you! Peace be to you, and peace be to your house, and peace be to all that you have. Now I have heard that you have shearers. Your shepherds have been with us, and we didn't harm them, neither was there anything missing from them, all the while they were in Carmel. Ask your young men, and they will tell you. Therefore let the young men find favor in your eyes; for we come on a good day. Please give whatever comes to your hand, to your servants, and to your son David.'"

When David's young men came, they spoke to Nabal all those words in the name of David and waited.

Nabal answered David's servants, and said, "Who is David? Who is the son of Jesse? There are many servants who break away from their masters these days. Shall I then take my bread, my water, and my meat that I have killed for my shearers, and give it to men when I don't know where they come from?"

So David's young men returned and told David what Nabal said.

David said to his men, "Every man put on his sword!"

Every man put on his sword. David also put on his sword. About four hundred men followed David, and two hundred stayed by the baggage. But one of the young men told Abigail, Nabal's wife, "Look, David sent messengers out of the wilderness to greet our master, and he insulted them. But the men were very good to us. As long as we went with them while we were in the fields, we were not harmed, and we didn't miss anything. While we were with them keeping the sheep they were a wall around us both by night and by day. Now consider what you will do for harm threatens our master and against all his house for he is such a worthless fellow no one can speak to him."

Then Abigail hurried and took 200 loaves of bread, two bottles of wine, five dressed sheep, five measures of roasted grain, 100 clusters of raisins, and 200 fig cakes, and put them on donkeys. She said to her young men, "Go on before me. I am coming after you." But she didn't tell her husband, Nabal. As she rode on her donkey, hidden by the hills, David and his men came down toward her, and she met them.

Now David had said, "In vain have I kept all
that this fellow has in the wilderness, so that
nothing was missed of all he had. He has returned me evil for good. Godde do so to the enemies of David, and more also, if by the morning
light, of all that belongs to him, I leave so much
as one who urinates on a wall."

When Abigail saw David, she quickly got off
of her donkey, and fell before David on her face,
bowing herself to the ground. She fell at his feet
and said, "On me, my lord, on me be the blame!
Please let your servant speak to you. Hear the
words of your servant. Please don't let my lord
pay attention to this worthless fellow, Nabal;
for as his name is, so is he. Nabal is his name,
and folly is with him. But I, your servant, didn't
see my lord's young men, whom you sent. Now
therefore, my lord, as Yahweh lives, and as your
soul lives, since Yahweh has withheld you from
the guilt of blood, and from avenging yourself
with your own hand, now let your enemies, and
those who seek evil to my lord, be as Nabal. Now
this present which your servant has brought to
my lord, let it be given to the young men who
follow my lord. Please forgive the trespass of
your servant. For Yahweh will certainly make
my lord a sure house, because my lord fights
Yahweh's battles. Evil will not be found in you all
your days. Though men may rise up to pursue
you and seek your life, yet my lord's life will be
bound in the bundle of life with Yahweh your
Godde. Yahweh will sling out the souls of your
enemies as from the hollow of a sling. It will
come to pass, when Yahweh has done to my
lord according to all the good that Yahweh has
spoken concerning you, and has appointed you
prince over Israel, that this shall be no grief to
you, nor offense of heart to my lord, either that

you have shed blood without cause, or that my lord has avenged himself. When Yahweh has dealt well with my lord then remember your servant."

David said to Abigail, "Blessed is Yahweh, the Godde of Israel, who sent you today to meet me! Blessed is your discretion, and blessed are you, who have kept me today from the guilt of blood and from avenging myself with my own hand. For indeed, as Yahweh, the Godde of Israel, lives, who has withheld me from harming you, unless you had hurried and come to meet me, surely by the morning light there wouldn't have been left to Nabal so much as one who urinates on a wall."

David received from her hand what she had brought him. Then he said to her, "Go in peace to your house. I have listened to your voice and have granted your request."

Abigail came to Nabal who he held a feast in his house, like the feast of a king. Nabal's heart was merry within him, for he was very drunk. So she told him nothing until the morning light. In the morning when Nabal was sober his wife told him these things, and his heart died within him, and he became like a stone. About ten days later, Yahweh struck Nabal so that he died. When David heard that Nabal was dead, he said, "Blessed is Yahweh, who has pleaded the cause of my reproach from the hand of Nabal and has kept back his servant from evil. Yahweh has returned the evildoing of Nabal on his own head." David sent and asked Abigail to be his wife. When David's servants came to Abigail at Carmel, they said to her, "David has sent us to you, to take you as his wife."

She arose and bowed herself with her face to the earth and said, "Behold, your servant is a servant to wash the feet of the servants of my lord." Abigail hurried, rose, and rode on a donkey with five ladies of hers who followed her, and she went after the messengers of David and became his wife.

—1 Samuel 25:2–42

More conservative branches of Evangelicalism believe that a wife should submit to her husband in all things. She should obey him unless he specifically tells her to sin.

1. What would have happened to Nabal's household if Abigail blindly submitted to him?

2. What would've happened if she said "Nabal is the head of the house, and I must submit to his headship"?

3. What do you learn about Abigail in this story?

4. Does the storyteller (or David's reaction) state or even imply Abigail's actions were sinful because she did not submit to Nabal's arrogance?

You never hear Abigail's story from complementarians who believe that wives should submit in all ways to their husbands, whether it's right or wrong. If Abigail had submitted in all ways to her fool of a husband (Nabal literally means "Fool" in Hebrew; translated as "surely" in this version), she would have resigned herself to certain death and her entire household to destruction. Abigail took the initiative and acted to save herself and her household.

Abigail didn't panic when the servant told her what Nabal said. She didn't wring her hands and wonder what to do. She jumped into action: decisive action. The food she and her servants were preparing for the feast was quickly loaded onto donkeys. Abigail sent the donkeys with her servants with a promise she would be right behind them.

Abigail's arrival was fortuitous. David had just sworn an oath that he would kill "everyone who urinates on a wall" in Nabal's household. Abigail wasted no time dismounting and bowing before David.

The first thing Abigail said to David was "On me, my lord, on me be the blame!" She could be talking about the blame or guilt of Nabal's insult of David. But she could also be talking about the vow David had just made.

1. Reread Abigail's speech to David. What does Abigail's speech tell you about her?

2. Does Abigail remind you of a woman we've already studied?

3. If Abigail reminds you of the Wise Woman of Abel, do you think Abigail is also a Wise Woman who is protecting the heritage of Yahweh?

After Abigail protected her household with her hospitality, she then gave David a reason to protect himself. Here Abigail's wisdom became prophetic. She told David she knew he would be king of Israel (at this time David was on the run from Saul), and she didn't want anyone to be able to hold anything against him. If he killed Nabal and their household, there would be blood guilt. Nabal was a powerful and wealthy man in the southern part of Israel, and David could be accused of killing him and his family to gain power and further his own career. When David came into power, there should be no blood guilt or doubt that Godde had called him and made him king. She also assured David that Godde would take care of his enemies, and that Godde would deal with Nabal.

By the time Abigail finished her wise and prophetic speech, David's temper had cooled, and he realized how close he had come to jeopardizing his chance of being Israel's future king. He praised Abigail for her wise words and for her courage in coming out to meet him, so there would be no question of blood guilt when he took the throne.

1. What do you think of the way Nabal died?

2. What do you think of Abigail becoming David's third wife?

If Abigail had been the "biblical woman" Fundamentalists and complementarians hold up, her household would have been killed, and David's act of vengeance might have cost him the throne of Israel. But Abigail did not submit to her husband's actions, nor did she keep silent. She was a wise woman who could size up a situation and take quick action to avert disaster. How can the church think that the commands in 1 Corinthians and 1 Timothy for women to keep silent are for all time when Abigail resides in our canon?

Chapter 6

Priscilla

There he found a Jew named Aquila, a native of
Pontus, who had recently come from Italy with
his wife Priscilla, because Claudius had ordered
all Jews to leave Rome. Paul went to see them,
and, because he was of the same trade, he stayed
with them, and they worked together--by trade
they were tentmakers.
—Acts 18:2–3, NRSV

Now there came to Ephesus a Jew named Apollos,
a native of Alexandria. He was an eloquent man,
well-versed in the scriptures. He had been in-
structed in the Way of [Christ]; and he spoke
with burning enthusiasm and taught accurately
the things concerning Jesus, though he knew only
the baptism of John. He began to speak boldly in
the synagogue; but when Priscilla and Aquila
heard him, they took him aside and explained the
Way of God to him more accurately. And when
he wished to cross over to Achaia, the believers
encouraged him and wrote to the disciples to welcome him. On his arrival he greatly helped those
who through grace had become believers, for he
powerfully refuted the Jews in public, showing by
the scriptures that the Messiah is Jesus.
—Acts 18:24–28, NRSV

> Greet Prisca and Aquila, who work with me in
> Christ Jesus, and who risked their necks for my
> life, to whom not only I give thanks, but also all
> the churches of the Gentiles.
> —Romans 16:3–4, NRSV

> Greet Prisca and Aquila, and the household of
> Onesiphorus.
> —2 Timothy 4:19, NRSV

Do you notice anything when you read these verses? It's a small thing, but it was unheard of in the Greek and Roman world in which Paul and Luke wrote. The husband's name always came first in greetings and listings. Always. It's the same in the Bible--both testaments. You just don't see the wife's name first. Except when the woman is Priscilla (or "Prisca," the shortened version of "Priscilla," like "Jennifer" and "Jenny"). Priscilla was the only wife to be listed ahead of her husband in the Bible.

1. What does this tell you about how the early church thought of Priscilla?

For the early church, Priscilla was the more important one in the couple. This is what one of the Church Fathers, John Chrysostom, wrote about the couple approximately 350 years after the New Testament:

> This too is worthy of inquiry, why, as he ad-
> dressed them, Paul has placed Priscilla before
> her husband. For he did not say, "Greet Aquila
> and Priscilla," but "Priscilla and Aquila." He does
> not do this without a reason, but he seems to me
> to acknowledge a greater godliness for her than
> for her husband. What I said is not guess-work,
> because it is possible to learn this from the Book
> of Acts. [Priscilla] took Apollos, an eloquent man
> and powerful in the Scriptures, but knowing only

> the baptism of John; and she instructed him in
> the way of [Yahweh] and made him a teacher
> brought to completion (Acts 18:24–25) (*First
> Homily on the Greeting to Priscilla and Aquila*).

Priscilla's name was listed first because Priscilla was the leader. She took the lead in teaching Apollos (a man who put himself under a woman's authority), and Aquila didn't seem to mind that his wife was the religious leader. Because of this tradition of Priscilla being the teacher, scholars have also speculated that Priscilla was the leader of the churches that met in their homes all over the Roman Empire: Corinth, Rome, and Ephesus. Priscilla and Aquila moved regularly around the Roman Empire to make a living weaving and selling tents, and they took their faith with them. This also meant Priscilla was bi-vocational: she was a tradeswoman who made tents, and a missionary and teacher as well. To those today who say a woman's sole place is in the home to be a mother and wife, Priscilla would laugh. She knew better: she knew a woman can be a wife and mother, along with having a career and a ministry. After all, she did all those things.

Paul's letter to the Corinthians was written before his letter to the Romans, which endorsed the ministry of Priscilla (see Romans 16:3).

1. Did Paul contradict himself?
2. Does that mean the command in 1 Corinthians was specifically for a situation in that congregation?

Priscilla and Aquila are also greeted at the end of 2 Timothy, and Priscilla's name comes first.

1. Is the writer of 1 and 2 Timothy contradicting himself?
2. Or is he writing to a specific problem in the church at Ephesus?

Part 3

Women in Authority
(Even over Men)

Chapter 7

Deborah

The children of Israel again did evil in Yahweh's sight after Ehud died. Yahweh sold them into the hand of Jabin king of Canaan, who reigned in Hazor. The captain of his army was Sisera, who lived in Harosheth of the Gentiles. The children of Israel cried to Yahweh, for he had nine hundred chariots of iron, and he greatly oppressed the children of Israel for twenty years. Now Deborah, a prophet, the wife of Lappidoth, judged Israel at that time. She lived under Deborah's palm tree between Ramah and Bethel in the hill country of Ephraim, and the children of Israel came up to her for judgment. She sent and called Barak the son of Abinoam out of Kedesh Naphtali, and said to him, "Hasn't Yahweh, the Godde of Israel, commanded, 'Go and lead the way to Mount Tabor, and take with you ten thousand men of the children of Naphtali and of the children of Zebulun? By the river Kishon I will draw Sisera, the captain of Jabin's army to you with his chariots and his troops. I will deliver him into your hand.'"

Barak said to her, "If you will go with me, then I will go, but if you will not go with me, I will not go."

She said, "I will go with you. Nevertheless, the journey that you take won't be for your honor

for Yahweh will sell Sisera into a woman's hand."
Deborah arose and went with Barak to Kedesh.

Barak called Zebulun and Naphtali together
to Kedesh, and ten thousand men followed him.
Deborah went up with him. Now Heber the
Kenite had separated himself from the Kenites,
even from the children of Hobab, Moses' brother-in-law, and pitched his tent as far as the oak
in Zaanannim, which is by Kedesh. They told
Sisera that Barak the son of Abinoam had gone
up to Mount Tabor. Sisera gathered together
all his chariots--nine hundred chariots of iron-
-and all the people who were with him, from
Harosheth of the Gentiles to the river Kishon.

Deborah said to Barak, "Go! For this is the
day in which Yahweh has delivered Sisera into
your hand. Hasn't Yahweh gone out before you?"
So Barak went down from Mount Tabor, and
ten thousand men after him. Yahweh confused
Sisera, all his chariots, and all his army with the
edge of the sword before Barak. Sisera abandoned
his chariot and fled away on foot. But Barak pur-
sued the chariots and the army to Harosheth of
the Gentiles, and all the army of Sisera fell by the
edge of the sword. There was no one left.
—Judges 4:1–16

The first three verses of this chapter are typical for the
book of Judges. In the book of Judges, Israel is caught
in a very destructive cycle. They decide to worship the
gods and goddesses around them instead of Yahweh–the
Godde who brought them out Egypt. Godde then gives
them over to an enemy who oppresses them for a while–
in this case, 20 years. Then the people come to their senses
and cry out to Godde who then raises a judge to deliver
them from their oppressors. There is much rejoicing and
the people obey Godde during the life of that judge, and

then the cycle starts all over again. This is called a downward spiral because not only does the same cycle keep happening, but each time it gets worse.

This story is a little different than the stories that have come before it. "Deborah, a prophet, wife of Lappidoth, judged Israel at the time" (Judges 4:4). Now we come to the first twist in this story–the judge was not a man, but a woman. We have an unlikely judge–she was a wife and probably a mother. Why was she the judge and not her husband? Because Godde called her and not him. Yes, it's as simple as that. And what about Lappidoth? I always wonder about this man. He's only mentioned once in the Bible, but he intrigues me. Since Deborah is judging Israel at the palm of Deborah and fulfilling her calling as a prophet, I'm assuming he's okay with the arrangement. Yes, in our day and age, we say "Well, duh, yes–she can work if she wants to." Back then, in that day and age, Deborah should have been toiling at home as a good wife and mother–cooking, cleaning, taking care of the kids. The place she should not have been was out in public, resolving disputes among the people. That was man's work. That should have been what Lappidoth was doing. But this unlikely couple obeyed Godde's rather strange calling on their lives–Godde called Deborah to be a prophet and judge, and both she and Lappidoth obeyed Godde's calling. This is why you will never hear complementarians talk about this couple. They blew the theory of gender roles out of the water way back in 1200 B.C.E.

The next person to enter our story is Barak, the general and commander of Israel's army. Deborah sent for him and told him Godde had spoken and wanted Barak to take an army and move against Israel's oppressor: Sisera. Now up to this point the men Godde called to judge Israel's enemies have been gung-ho about going and wreaking a little havoc. Godde told them to go and destroy Israel's enemies, and they went and destroyed Israel's enemies in some very creative ways with no cajoling or prodding. When Deborah called Barak and told him Godde was ready to move against Sisera, we expect Barak to yell, "Yippee, it's about time!" and go. But that's not what he did. Barak placed a condition on his obedience: Deborah must go with him. The general wanted a woman to accompany him in battle. And this woman, this married women who probably had children, said yes. If that's what it took to do Godde's will then she would go, so that the enemy could be defeated.

But Barak's condition cost him—he would not be the one to kill Sisera; in another irony of the story, a woman would be the one to kill Sisera.

I don't think we should be too hard on Barak for wanting Deborah to go with him. Remember Deborah was a prophet: she was Godde's representative on earth, speaking the words Godde gave her. I think if I was Barak, I might want her to come along too. It also was a common thing for a prophet or seer to go with the army into battle to tell the general the best time to attack because the prophet would know when the god/s wanted them to attack. Barak wanting a prophet to go to war with him was not that unusual.

Word came to Sisera that Barak and the Israelite troops were on the move, and Sisera went out to meet them, thinking he had this battle won. But Godde had other plans. Deborah gave the command for the troops to march, and Barak led the way. As they were moving toward each other, Godde threw Sisera's army into a panic, and the Israelites defeated the Canaanites.

There are people who have problems with this passage because a woman led an army into battle. Some have problems because they think that is a man's job. Others don't like this because they think women should find peaceful ways of resolving conflicts and not giving into what they consider to be male violence.

1. How do you feel about a woman leading a male army into battle?

2. What do you think of Lappidoth who had no problems with his wife being a leader of their people and had no trouble with her leading an army into battle?

3. Do you think Barak was weak for wanting a woman to accompany him in battle?

4. What do Deborah's actions say about Godde?

What does this story tell you about what Godde thinks of women in leadership positions over both men and women in both the sacred and secular realms (prophet and judge/military leader)?

Like Abigail, Deborah is a woman complementarians don't like to talk about. If they do talk about her, they say Godde called a woman to lead because all the men were disobedient and not doing what Godde told them to do (like Barak who wouldn't go to war without Deborah). Godde lowered the standards because a woman was all Godde had to work with.

The only problem with this interpretation is that there is nothing in the story to back it up. The people who went to Deborah with their problems didn't act like it was a big deal to go to a female judge. Barak did not act surprised that a female prophet told him to go to war. He only wanted the assurance of Godde's presence Deborah represented with him when he went. The narrator of the story did not seem to think it was unusual for a woman to be spiritual and secular leader, so why should we?

Chapter 8

Huldah

Hilkiah the high priest said to Shaphan the scribe, "I have found the book of the law in Yahweh's house." Hilkiah delivered the book to Shaphan, and he read it. Shaphan the scribe came to the king, and brought the king word again, and said, "Your servants have emptied out the money that was found in the house and delivered it into the hand of the workers who have oversight of Yahweh's house." Shaphan the scribe told the king, saying, "Hilkiah the priest has delivered a book to me." Shaphan read it before the king. When the king heard the words of the book of the law, he tore his clothes. The king commanded Hilkiah the priest, and Ahikam the son of Shaphan, and Achbor the son of Micaiah, and Shaphan the scribe, and Asaiah the king's servant, saying, "Go inquire of Yahweh for me, and for the people, and for all Judah about the words of this book that has been found. For the wrath of Yahweh is greatly kindled against us because our ancestors have not listened to the words of this book, obeying all that is written to us."

So Hilkiah the priest, and Ahikam, and Achbor, and Shaphan and Asaiah went to Huldah the prophetess, the wife of Shallum the

son of Tikvah, the son of Harhas, keeper of the wardrobe (now she lived in Jerusalem in the second quarter), and they talked with her. She said to them, "Yahweh, the Godde of Israel, says: 'Tell the man who sent you to me, "Yahweh says, 'Behold, I will bring evil on this place, and on its inhabitants, even all the words of the book which the king of Judah has read. Because they have forsaken me, and have burned incense to other gods, that they might provoke me to anger with all the work of their hands, therefore my wrath shall be kindled against this place, and it shall not be quenched.'" But to the king of Judah, who sent you to inquire of Yahweh, you shall tell him, "Yahweh, the Godde of Israel, says: 'Concerning the words which you have heard, because your heart was tender, and you humbled yourself before Yahweh, when you heard what I spoke against this place and against its inhabitants–that they should become a desolation and a curse, and have torn your clothes, and wept before me–I also have heard you,' says Yahweh. 'Look, I will gather you to your ancestors, and you shall be gathered to your grave in peace, neither shall your eyes see all the evil which I will bring on this place.'" They brought back this message to the king.
—2 Kings 22:8–20

Did you know that the first person to declare written words as Scripture was a woman?

Her name was Huldah, and she was a prophet in Jerusalem during the reign of King Josiah. Her story is found in 2 Kings 22 and 2 Chronicles 34. During his reign, Josiah tried to bring the people of Judah back to the worship of Yahweh, the one true Godde. He had idols thrown out of the temple, then he authorized repairs to the temple. During the renovations a scroll was found and brought to the high priest and king. Neither one knew if it was Godde's word. Josiah ordered the high priest to take the scroll to a prophet. Although there were noteworthy male prophets in Jerusalem at the time–Jeremiah, Zephaniah, and Nahum–Josiah sent the high priest to inquire of a female prophet, Huldah. Huldah verified the scroll was the word of Godde, and that its prophecies would happen. The scroll said that if Israel did not worship only Yahweh as Godde, they would lose their land and be sent into exile. Death and destruction would be the result of their disobedience. Huldah verified the Jewish people had passed the point of no return: both Jerusalem and the temple would be destroyed. But Josiah would be spared war and exile since his heart was grieved over the sin of his people. Huldah's prophecy was fulfilled within 35 years of this event. After Josiah heard her words, he stepped up his reforms and led the people in celebrating the first Passover that included all of the people since before the time of the judges (2 Kings 23:22).

1. What do you think of a woman being the first to declare the written word as Scripture?

2. Do you think it might affect how you read the Bible from now on?

Huldah was the first person to declare written words to be the word of Godde–Scripture. She was the first whose "words of judgment are centered on a written document as no others have been before her".[1] She was the first to authenticate Scripture. Manuscripts had accumulated for years, if not centuries, but for the first time a prophet

1. Claudia V. Camp, *Women's Bible Commentary*, 115.

proclaimed the written word to be Godde's word, and this prophet was a woman–the last female prophet before Judah fell to the Babylonians. Huldah started the process that would eventually give us canonized Scripture.

Efforts to marginalize Huldah's leadership role claim her authority came from her husband. Huldah was married to Shallum who was the "keeper of the wardrobe" (2 Kings 22:14)—a royal position. But when the high priest and his entourage came to her home, they did not ask for her husband. According to Scripture, these men were not embarrassed asking a woman about Godde's will for their country. The high priest did not have an issue with a woman prophet. In fact, her gender was irrelevant in the story, as was her marital status. Huldah was a religious leader in Jerusalem at that time, and the high priest had no problem going to her to confirm Godde's word.

Chapter 9

Phoebe

> I commend to you our sister Phoebe, a deacon
> of the community at Cenchreae, so that you may
> welcome her in the Lady as holy ones should
> and help her with whatever she needs, because
> she has been a patron of many, and of me too.
> —Romans 16:1–2

1. What words does Paul use to describe Phoebe?

2. What do you think of Paul calling a woman a deacon?

3. Did you grow up with deacons in your local church?
   Who were they? What determined if people could
   hold those positions?

Paul introduces Phoebe as a deacon. What's odd is
that, in the Greek, a masculine form of the word is used to
describe a woman. It was the same word Paul used when
he called Timothy and Titus "servants" or "deacons" (or
ministers) of their respective churches. Another thing
makes this phrase odd: Phoebe is called the "deacon of
the church of Cenchreae." This is the only place in the
New Testament where the term "deacon" is followed by a
specific congregation. This is the only place linking a spe-

cific person's ministry with a specific church. This seems
to indicate that Phoebe served as a minister or pastor in
the church at Cenchreae.

Paul used another word to describe Phoebe: *prostatēs*
or patron. This is the only occurrence of the word in
the New Testament. It is normally translated so its
main meaning is not obvious. The normal translation is
"helper" or someone who has helped. The basic and most
obvious translation of the word from classical Greek is
"patron" or "benefactor," and women in this role are well
attested in the Roman world. In the Greco-Roman world
wealthy women sponsored the arts, philosophers, writers, and politicians. The patrons paid the artists, politicians, or missionaries and gave them the social standing
they needed to succeed. Phoebe was a wealthy woman
who served the church out of her means as the women
in Luke 8:1–3 served Jesus out of theirs. For Paul to say
Phoebe was his benefactor meant she helped to finance
his missionary travels. It's also very likely she was known
in Rome, and she had the appropriate social status and
clout to introduce Paul to the churches there. Paul did
not start the churches in Rome, and he had not visited
these churches. It was important for the right person with
the right connections and influence to introduce him to
the Roman churches. He wanted those churches to be
a base for his further missionary work into Spain. Paul
entrusted Phoebe with his letter of introduction in hopes
that her social status would compel the churches in Rome
to help him on to Spain.

Phoebe was a wealthy and independent woman who
served the church as a deacon/pastor and in using her
money and social connections to further the mission
of the church. Paul came very close to commanding

churches he had no hand in planting, and Christians, most of whom he never met, to welcome her and provide anything she needed. She was not only a deacon and a benefactor in the church, but Paul himself had also benefited from her generous leadership.

1. What do you think of a woman financially supporting a man?

2. What do you think of Paul commending Phoebe to the Romans with such great praise and admitting she had given money to him and supported him in his missionary endeavors?

3. Do you think Paul would limit women the way complementarians claim he did while endorsing Phoebe this way?

Preface to Chapters 10 & 11

BEFORE WE DIVE INTO the chapters on those eight little verses in 1 Corinthians and 1 Timothy, we need a little background on those letters. 1 Corinthians and 1 Timothy are letters written to two different churches: one in Corinth and the other in Ephesus. We know Paul wrote 1 Corinthians. Paul could have written 1 Timothy. But it is doubtful the church during Paul's time had the organization and hierarchy which are talked about in 1 Timothy: there just hadn't been that much time to organize (the church was only 30–35 years old when Paul was martyred). Plus for most of Paul's life either Rome or the Jewish synagogue persecuted the church, and the early Christians would've been more concerned with finding safe places to worship than how to structure church hierarchy. I don't think Paul wrote 1 and 2 Timothy or Titus. Don't worry: I won't be using that as an excuse to gloss over the verses in 1 Timothy 2 by claiming they are not really Scripture. 1 Timothy is part of our canon and must be respected as Scripture, which is how I will treat it.

Chapter 10

The Corinthian Church

Here are some of the problems Paul was dealing with in his first letter to the churches at Corinth: a man was sleeping with his stepmother; there were rivalries and factions in the church; one group thought it was better because of who they had come into the church under. In my view, the most despicable problem was the way the Corinthians were conducting their "agape feasts" or love feasts. In the early days of the church, communion was part of a bigger meal involving the whole church community. In 1 Corinthians 11:20–22 Paul castigates the Corinthian believers: "So when you come together you're not really eating the Lord's supper because when you eat, everyone eats their own supper first. One goes hungry and another gets drunk. What, don't you have houses to eat and drink in? Or do you underestimate Godde's community and shame those who don't have anything? What should I tell you? Should I praise you? I won't praise you about this."

The richer members of the church came to the feast early, then ate and drank themselves into a stupor. When the peasants and slaves came after they were done working, there was nothing left. The poorest in the community were going hungry because the rich members were gluttons.

Sexual immorality, fights, factions, divisions, and no regard for the poorer members of the congregation were some of the problems that Paul dealt with in the Corinthian church. This letter needs to be read as a collection of specific instructions to a specific group, and parts of this letter are not going to translate to absolute principles to be obeyed for all of eternity. We no longer have community meals before communion in most churches. Although the advice on rivalries and divisions are still very apt for today's church, discernment is needed.

Where does that leave the instructions for women in this letter? First we need to remember what instructions to women boil down to in the New Testament: women were property of men. They were first the property of their fathers, then the property of their husbands. Any instruction given to women assumed women were literally owned by their husbands. Instructions to husbands and wives assumed the husband owned everything: wife (or wives), children, servants, and slaves were all the property of the head of the household, the man. That was the foundation of all instructions given to women, not in only the New Testament, but in the whole Bible.

How women should act in church gets more confusing the further we read in 1 Corinthians. Paul dealt with several issues regarding women and worship: whether or not married women should have their heads covered, as well as suggestions made for women who prayed and prophesied during the service. Wait, you may be wondering, didn't Paul say women could not speak at all in church? But he also gave instructions for how women are to pray and prophesy?

Before we come to our verses in 1 Corinthians 14, Paul deals with women praying and prophesying during the worship service and whether or not they should have their heads covered in 1 Corinthians 11:2–16. Paul does not condemn women for taking an active part in the service, including authoritative prophetic utterance of Godde's word. There are two different ways to interpret the instructions Paul gives in these verses. Let's look at this passage from the New Revised Standard Version:

> I commend you because you remember me in everything and maintain the traditions just as I handed them on to you. But I want you to understand that Christ is the head of every man, and the husband is the head of his wife, and God is the head of Christ. Any man who prays or prophesies with something on his head disgraces his head, but any woman who prays or prophesies with her head unveiled disgraces her head—it is one and the same thing as having her head shaved. For if a woman will not veil herself, then she should cut off her hair; but if it is disgraceful for a woman to have her hair cut off or to be shaved, she should wear a veil. For a man ought not to have his head veiled, since he is the image and reflection of God; but woman is the reflection of man. Indeed, man was not made from woman, but woman from man. Neither was man created for the sake of woman, but woman for the sake of man. For this reason a woman ought to have a symbol of authority on her head, because of the angels. Nevertheless, in the Lord woman is not independent of man or man independent of woman. For just as woman came from man, so man comes through woman; but all things come from God. Judge for yourselves: is it proper for a woman to pray to God with her head unveiled? Does not nature itself teach you that if a man wears long hair, it

> is degrading to him, but if a woman has long
> hair, it is her glory? For her hair is given to her
> for a covering. But if anyone is disposed to be
> contentious—we have no such custom, nor do
> the churches of God.
> —1 Corinthians 11:2–16

The first way to interpret these verses is that Paul exhorts the women to pray and prophesy in a manner that will not be scandalous to outsiders. If they are married, they are to keep their symbol of marriage on–their head was to be covered with a veil or worn up, as was the custom for married women in that day. This way they would not be confused with the temple prostitutes who were numerous in Corinth due to the temple of Aphrodite-Melainis. The temple prostitutes were identified by wearing their hair loose or shaving it off. Christian women were not to bring shame onto their husbands by looking like prostitutes, but were to keep their "wedding rings" on, and prophesy and pray in a socially acceptable manner.

The second way to interpret these verses is that Paul is countering a custom in the Corinthian church that he does not consider to be Christian. Now let's look at these same verses from the Divine Feminine Version:

> Now I praise you because you remember me in
> everything and firmly hold the traditions just as
> I passed them on to you.
>   But I want you to know that the head of every
> man is Christ, and the head of the woman is
> the man, and the head of Christ is God. Every
> man who prays or prophesies with anything
> on his head shames his head. But every woman
> who prays or prophesies with her head unveiled
> shames her head, because it's the same as hav-

ing her head shaved. If a woman isn't veiled, she should cut off her hair. But if it's shameful for a woman to have her hair cut off or her head shaved, she should be veiled. A man shouldn't have his head veiled since he's the image and glory of God, but the woman is the glory of the man because the man wasn't made from the woman, but the woman from the man. The man wasn't created for the woman, but the woman for the man.

But the woman should have liberty over her head for this reason: because of the angels. The point is that in the Lady, the woman isn't independent of the man, nor is the man independent of the woman, because just as woman came from man, so a man comes through a woman too, but all things are from Godde. Judge for yourselves. "Is it appropriate for a woman to pray to Godde unveiled?" Isn't it natural to think that if a man has long hair, it's dishonorable for him, but if a woman has long hair, it's a glory to her? Because her hair has been given to her instead of a veil. But if anyone wants to quarrel, we have no such custom, nor do Godde's communities.

When we read the verses this way the Corinthians were the ones who wanted to impose a gender hierarchy and limit the freedom that women have in Christ. But Paul counters that women, like men, will judge the angels, and that whether her head is covered is irrelevant because nature has given women a natural covering: their hair. Women were free to pray and prophesy however they wanted because "a woman ought to have liberty over her head." Paul also countered the argument that Godde created man to be the head of the woman so that women were just "the image of man," not made in "the image of

Godde" as men were. But Paul said that men and women are interdependent because although Godde made woman from man, nevertheless, since the first woman, men come from women, and both sexes were created by Godde. If we translate these verses in this way then there is no contradiction with what Paul wrote in Galatians 3:28: There is no longer male or female because we are all one in Christ.

From these verses we know that when Paul later says "It is shameful for a woman to speak in church" he could not mean all speech, because he just endorsed women praying and prophesying in the church. He not only endorsed women speaking but women as leaders in their congregations.

Now let's take a look at those verses that supposedly say it is shameful for a woman to speak in church. Here are the verses from the NRSV:

> For God is a God not of disorder but of peace. (As in all the churches of the saints, women should be silent in the churches. For they are not permitted to speak, but should be subordinate, as the law also says. If there is anything they desire to know, let them ask their husbands at home. For it is shameful for a woman to speak in church. Or did the word of God originate with you? Or are you the only ones it has reached?) (1 Corinthians 14:33–36).

As with the passage from chapter 11, these verses could be Paul correcting a non-Christian Corinthian belief. Here is another way to translate these verses:

> Godde isn't a Godde of confusion, but of peace, as in all the communities of the holy ones.

> Women should keep quiet in the communities, because they aren't allowed to speak; but they should be submissive, as the Torah says. If they want to learn anything, they should ask their own husbands at home, because it's shameful for a woman to speak in the community.
>
> What? Did the message of Godde originate with you? Or are you the only ones it reached? (1 Corinthians 14:33–35, DFV).

We know Paul did not mean this for all women for all time because of the verses in chapter 11. We know women were praying and prophesying–speaking and speaking with authority–in the church. There are two different ways to translate these verses, and three different ways we can interpret these verses.

First there are textual variations in the text. What does that mean? It means that in different ancient manuscripts, these verses appear in different places. In most manuscripts, verses 33–36 are where they are in modern English versions of the Bible. But in some ancient manuscripts, verses 33–36 appear at the end of chapter 14. These inconsistencies show the early church did not agree on where these verses belonged, meaning they could have been added later. As the church continued to grow and it became more important to appeal to those outside of the church, cultural norms that were not originally imposed on women now were, for the sake of appearance. Someone was uneasy about the freedom Paul gave women in 1 Corinthians and edited it to make it look like the apostle forbade women to speak. He should've corrected 11:2–16 while he was at it for consistency's sake. These verses may not have been in the original letter.

If you believe Paul wrote these verses, there are two other ways to explain this discrepancy. Paul was talking about another situation altogether from preaching and prophesying. Paul and the Corinthian church knew what the issue was, but we don't. We have to make "educated guesses." One of the best of those guesses is this one. In Jewish synagogues, men sat on one side of the room and women on the other side of the room. Jewish converts brought this custom with them to the church. In both Jewish and Greco-Roman culture, women were not educated. For the first time in their lives many women were able to sit and learn about faith and religion. They had questions. Apparently they were yelling their questions across the room to their husbands who would then yell back responses. It would be hard to concentrate on the speaker with all of that ruckus going on. Paul is telling the women to save their questions for when they get home, then ask their husbands. In this case, Paul is saying that it is shameful for women to yell across the room at their husbands in church. That makes a lot of sense.

The third way we can deal with these verses is that "Let wives keep quiet in the communities, because they aren't allowed to speak; but let them be submissive like the Torah says. If they want to learn anything, let them ask their own husbands at home, because it's a shame for a woman to talk in the community" is what the Corinthian men believed, and Paul was telling them they were wrong, just as he told them they were wrong in chapter 11, regarding the creation and roles of men and women. His response to this absurd view of women staying silent in the church is "What? Did the word of Godde originate with you? Or are you the only ones it reached?" In other words: in other churches women were not silent, and it was not shameful for women to speak in church. Paul is not letting the Corinthian church silence women or hamper their roles in leadership as prophets and prayers.

Whether you believe these verses were written by Paul or added later, it's obvious, when put in the context of the whole letter, Paul did not mean for these verses to be applied to all women for all time. They were either a correction to non-Christian Corinthian belief, or they were for some women to take care of a specific problem in the church. They also could have been added later to "correct" Paul and make sure women kept their place as silent property of men in the church.

Chapter 11

The Ephesian Church

1 TIMOTHY IS ANOTHER letter written to a church with multiple problems. Ephesus was a tough place to pastor a church. It was the site of one of the seven wonders of the world: the temple of Diana. The cult of Diana had great power and influence in the city. Like Corinth, Ephesus was also a crossroads of the Roman Empire both by sea and by land. It was a metropolitan city that liked its many gods and goddesses and its multiculturalism. Out of all the gods, Diana was the queen and the patron of the city. Priestesses in the cult of Diana wielded great power both in and out of the temple. Men who were part of the cult were either sacred prostitutes or eunuchs dedicated to Diana.[1] They did not hold power. Only female priestesses could be leaders in the cult. The cult of Diana also believed woman was created first and then man, and they taught that men should be in subjection to women.

Many religions flourished in Ephesus, and these religions with their varied beliefs made their way into the Ephesian church. The author of this letter is first and foremost concerned with doctrinal purity and weeding out what he considered heresy. This letter to a young

1. See Catherine and Richard Clark Kroeger, *I Suffer Not a Woman*, 94–98.

pastor in Ephesus is concerned with sound doctrine and decorum. He believed the household, as a unit, was the stability of society, and since churches met in homes, the church needed to follow the strict rules of the Greco-Roman household. Once again this meant that women were seen as property of the husband.

The working hypothesis for my interpretation of 1 Timothy 2:11–15 is that women, who were formerly priestesses of Diana, were becoming Christians and bringing their attitude of female superiority with them. These women obviously did not believe in the Greco-Roman (and quickly becoming Christian) attitude of patriarchalism with women being totally subservient to men. Their former temple put that ancient belief on its head. I believe they were teaching the women in the church not to be submissive and to claim their leader-ship abilities by subjugating men just as the priestesses of Diana had done in their own cult. The writer of this epistle wanted to reign in both heresy and the power these women had. He also wanted to make the church more appealing to the metropolitan Gentiles of Ephesus by reinforcing patriarchal family values. These verses are how he did it:

> Let a woman learn in silence with full submis-sion. I permit no woman to teach or to have authority over a man; she is to keep silent. For Adam was formed first, then Eve; and Adam was not deceived, but the woman was deceived and became a transgressor. Yet she will be saved through childbearing, provided they continue in faith and love and holiness, with modesty (1 Timothy 2:11–15, NRSV).

> There is a woman who needs to quietly receive instruction in submission. I don't want her to teach or to upstage her husband, but to keep quiet, because Adam was formed first, then Eve; and Adam wasn't tricked, but Eve was tricked and became a lawbreaker; and women who have children will be given life, provided they continue in trust, love, and holiness with self-restraint (1 Timothy 2:11–15, DFV).

See how different these verses look in the the Divine Feminine Version compared with the New Revised Standard Version? These verses can appear pretty cut and dry, but, as you can see, there are vastly different ways these verses can be translated. To begin with there are two keywords that can be interpreted in a variety of ways. The first one is the word that is translated as "silence." The Greek word is *hesuchios*, and it's basic meaning is to live "a quiet and peaceful life."[2] In 1 Peter it is used to describe "a meek and quiet spirit," and in 1 Thessalonians 4:11 it's used to show that Christians should live lives that are "quiet [and to] mind your own affairs." *Hesuchios* also "implies compliance with the law rather than resistance, and harmony with one's neighbors rather than wrangling and hostility."[3] The word doesn't necessarily mean "shut up."

The next word which has many meanings and nuances is the word translated as "authority over." *Authentēs* is a squirrely word in the Greek. It has a wide variety of meanings, and like all language and words, changes meaning from generation to generation. The range of meanings include "murderer," "usurping authority," "domineering," and "originator." It is also used to show the absolute au-

2. Ibid., 68.
3. Ibid.

thority wielded by a monarch or god. The Greek translation of the Old Testament and early Christian writers use *Authentēs* to describe Godde. Quite a range, huh? It can mean authority like that of a teacher or leader, but normally it has abusive or sovereign nuances. Most uses of the word are not positive.[4]

The writer of 1 Timothy could be prohibiting women from usurping authority from recognized church leaders (probably male). The former Dianic priestesses, lead by one particular woman the writer had in mind, could have been fighting and arguing for the preeminence of women over men during worship services and teaching times. They were not taking the time to learn biblical belief, but were intent on forcing their views. These women and their leader needed to stop, listen, and learn correct doctrine in peace before they started arguing for their own ways.

There is another way to interpret these verses. Did you notice one word in the paragraph giving the range of meanings that didn't quite fit in? "Originator" looks a little out of place with all those power words. While one branch of the word group for *Authentēs* goes to the terms for abusive power, another branch gives us our word "authentic." This branch of words describes people who build, come up with an idea, or start something new. It can also refer to a government legislating a new law. With this definition Richard and Catherine Clark Kroeger offer this alternative translation: "I do not permit woman to teach nor to represent herself as originator of man

---

4. For the full range of what *authentēs* can mean see Richard and Catherine Clark Kroeger's *I Suffer Not a Woman*, chapter 7: "That Strange Greek Verb Authentein" and Appendix 1: "Could Authentein Mean Murder?"

but she is to be in conformity [with the Scriptures]. For Adam was created first, then Eve."[5]

This translation then flows nicely into why the author would bring up Adam and Eve in this section. In the Hebrew Scriptures Godde created man first then woman, so women shouldn't be coming into the church teaching that woman was created before man. We can see this view in the Gnostic text, "On the Origin of the World," which says

> "After the day of rest, Sophia sent her daughter Zoe, being called Eve, as an instructor, in order that she might make Adam, who had no soul, arise, so that those whom he should engender might become containers of light. When Eve saw her male counterpart prostrate, she had pity upon him, and she said, "Adam! Become alive! Arise upon the earth!" Immediately her word became accomplished fact. For Adam, having arisen, suddenly opened his eyes. When he saw her, he said, "You shall be called 'Mother of the Living'. For it is you who have given me life."
> [Nag Hammadi Collection II.5.115.31–34]

Given the Gnostic belief in woman giving man life, translating *Authentēs* as "originator" fits very nicely in these verses. According to Genesis, Godde created man first then woman. If only the letter writer had stopped there instead of giving a faulty interpretation of what Christians call the Fall: humanity's original sin.

We find the original account in Genesis 3, and there we find that the man and woman were together in the garden when the serpent tempted them. Both listened, both ate, and both sinned. The writer of 1 Timothy places

5. Ibid, 103.

blame for original sin squarely on the woman, unlike Paul, who held both Adam and Eve accountable for the first sin. In fact, Paul uses Adam's sin in Romans 5 to point out that just as sin came into the world through one man, redemption could come into the world through one man, Jesus Christ. To say Adam was not deceived, and place the blame squarely on Eve, goes against Genesis 3 and Paul's earlier interpretation of the Creation stories. Here the writer strays from the biblical tradition he is trying so hard to uphold.

And what of the last verse? "Yet she will be saved through childbearing, provided they continue in faith and love and holiness, with modesty. (1 Tim 2:15, NRSV).

The first question is who is the subject of this verse? We start out with the single person "she" at the beginning of the verse then switch to the plural "they" in the second half. Does it start talking about Eve (she) then expand to the women in the Ephesian congregation (they)? Is "she" a woman who was teaching incorrect doctrine, and the writer was reassuring "they," the women of the congregation? Along with the former priestesses of Diana, was there a Gnostic in the Ephesian church teaching that women shouldn't have children?

First what was Gnosticism? Gnosticism was a belief system that grew up alongside of Christianity that totally separated the flesh and spirit. Godde was Spirit and therefore could have nothing to do with the flesh. Gnostics believed that a lesser god made the material creation, and that it was evil. Any material, fleshy thing was evil, including the human body. One strain of Gnosticism believed that giving into fleshly desires like marriage and childbearing barred a person from moving on to heaven. They would be stuck in a lower level, quasi-spiritual place that they would have to work themselves out of. The only way to ensure clear passage to eternal life and the presence of Godde was to deny the body in all forms and remain celibate. One of the early Church Fathers, Clement of Alexandria, described and refuted this belief in the second century:

> Those who are opposed to God's creation, disparaging it under the fair name of continence, also quote the words to Salome which we mentioned earlier. They are found, I believe, in the Gospel according to the Egyptians. They say that the Saviour himself said "I came to destroy the works of the female," meaning by "female" desire, and by "works" birth and corruption [Clement of Alexandra, Stromatas III.9].

The writer reassured women that marriage and childbearing would not hamper their salvation or eternal life. He was reassuring women that they, too, were saved the same way as men: through faith in Christ and obeying his commands.

In the end we see that these four verses are not set in stone. First, no one is sure exactly how they should be translated. There are words which have multiple definitions, and we are not sure how they should be translated. These verses cannot be used as an all-time, all-encompassing principle for women because we don't know exactly what the writer meant. And like the first letter to the Corinthians, this letter was written to a troubled church with very specific problems. We should be hesitant to take instructions to these churches as permanent law, especially when they ban half of the Christian church from teaching and leading in the church.

Appendix 1

Bringing the Women of the Bible
Out from the Shadows

GROWING UP IN AN evangelical church, I heard some about the women of the Bible. Not much. Just enough to tell me that Godde's will for me was to grow up, get married, and have kids. That's what Christian women did. That's what the women in the Bible did. And sure enough, whenever I heard about the women in the Bible, they were wives and mothers, taking care of their families.

But submission of wives to husbands was not the only thing I learned growing up evangelical. I also learned how important it was to read the Bible and know what the Bible says. As far as I'm concerned, the "knowing your Bible" emphasis backfired on the movement with me. Because I started noticing something. I started noticing women weren't only wives and mothers. I learned women didn't always submit to their husbands. I learned there were single women in the Bible who never married or had children.

The women in the Bible I came to know through my own study were totally different women than I grew up with in Sunday Schools and sermons. These were tough women, strong women, and intelligent women. I found out women were judges, prophets, worship leaders, and business women. I found out a man would not go to war without a certain woman by his side. I found out women were evangelists, preachers, and patrons of the church. I found out these women had been set to the side and put in the shadows. They had been marginalized and ignored because they weren't simply wives and mothers. They showed women could be more, much more.

Thanks to women coming into Biblical studies and theology, these women's stories are being told. But we have a long way to go. So how do we go about bringing these women to center stage? How do we bring them out of the shadows?

How do we go about bringing the women of the Bible out of hiding?

The most important thing you can do is ask two questions: What does the story say? What doesn't the story say? We come to the Bible with layer on layer on layer of interpretations and tradition. We come to the Bible with layer upon layer of assumptions and other cultural norms being imposed on the story. We come with our own assumptions and cultural baggage. Reading and re-reading and reading again the story and seeing what's there and what isn't there is the most important thing we can do. In the process of reading and re-reading the story and asking "what does this story say," "what doesn't this story say," we begin to peel away the layers of interpretations and traditions and assumptions. We begin to see the cultural baggage of our own time and past times that have been hung on the story.

This is particularly important when reading the stories of biblical women. A lot of cultural baggage regarding what women are supposed to be like gets attached to these women. We've seen this again and again with the women we have studied in this book.

Deborah gets buried under a lot of baggage (Judges 4). The part of Christianity that believes women were made to be helpers to their husbands, that women are to be submissive wives and mothers, do not like Deborah. They do one of two things to her: 1) they ignore her or 2) they explain away her leadership roles. If they have to admit Godde does call women to lead in both religious and civil settings (including leading men), they have to admit their interpretation of the Bible is wrong. Instead they marginalize the women leaders in the Bible, like Deborah. Here's how they diminish Deborah's role: 1) the only reason Deborah is a judge is because no man would step up to the plate. Deborah is Godde's last resort. 2) Deborah and Barak were married, so Barak was the leader and Deborah was his helpmate. 3) Deborah's husband Lappidoth was a commander with Barak, so Deborah is under her husband's authority.

This is why it's so important to read and re-read the story and see what is really there. And just importantly, to see what's not there. A lot of what we believe about biblical women and how Christian women should behave and act simply is not in the Bible. It's all been added on. Or the stories that back up the presuppositions are the ones we hear about while the rest are changed or ignored.

The second thing we need to realize is the Bible is all about action. The Bible is not all that interested in motives. In the Bible, you show who you are and what your motives are by what you do. Actions always take precedence over motive. When we look at the stories of the Biblical women, one of the first things we ask is what does this woman do? What are her actions? Then we ask, what do these actions say about the woman? And what do the woman's actions say about Godde?

After we ask what does the story say? What doesn't it say? And what do the actions in this story say? We look at the history and culture these women lived in, which changes throughout the Bible.

Women's and men's roles change from culture to culture and from one era to the next. During the time of the Hebrew Scriptures, it was the women's job to not only make the tents, but to put them up and then take them down again. So when we read in Judges 4 that tent pegs and a hammer are in Jael's tent in easy reach for her, this rings true. Of course the pegs and hammer would be in her tent; she assembled the tent and broke it down when it was time to move on. When the Israelites started settling down in houses, the men built them. But it was the woman's job to repair them by replacing bricks and fixing the roof. It may be considered man's work today, but 4,000 years ago, it was women's work. Gender roles do change from culture to culture and over time. They are not static.

Another thing we need to know is that the more the government is centralized, the less of a role a woman has in the public sphere. We saw this with Deborah: during the time of the tribes–a decentralized government–a woman could be a military leader. That will change with the monarchy. During the monarchy when power is centralized to the king, the priests, and the ruling elite, women leaders disappear. The only two woman leaders who really appear at this time are Jezebel and Huldah. Jezebel had power and knew how to use it, which is why I think she gets cast as "evil," idolatry and all (1 Kings 16:29–22:40; 2 Kings 9:30–37). At the end of the monarchy in Jerusalem Huldah appears, but she is a safe woman leader (2 Kings 22 and 2 Chronicles 34). She is married to the keeper of the wardrobe for the palace, so she is upper class. And she is a prophet, which was still a safe role for women. You would not find a Deborah during this time.

The last thing to remember about the Bible is that obedience is more important than cultural norms. Read that again: obedience is more important than cultural norms. The cultural norm in Egypt at the time Moses was born was to throw baby boys into the Nile (Exodus 1–2). Jochebed obeyed God by breaking both the law of the land and what was culturally expected of her. She was a slave; she was expected to obey her human rulers, period. She didn't. She obeyed Godde. In Genesis the cultural norm said it was the patriarch who decided who would be the next clan leader and the heir of the covenant with Godde. Issac was going to bless Esau and pass leadership on to him. But the matriarch, Rebekah, knew Jacob was the child of promise and the heir. So Rebekah became a trickster (a role that ran rampant in her family) and manipulated the situation so Jacob received the blessing (Genesis 27).

The three historical and cultural things to remember when reading these women's stories are: gender roles change, the more decentralized a government the more power women have in the public sphere, and in the Bible obedience is always more important than cultural norms.

Appendix 2

Bringing the Women of the Bible Out from the Shadows: A Cheat Sheet

Ask these questions:

1. What does the story say?

2. What doesn't the story say?

3. What does this woman do? What are her actions?

4. What do these actions say about the woman?

5. What do the woman's actions say about Godde?

Learn about biblical history and culture and remember:

1. Gender roles change from one culture to another and one age to the next.

2. The more centralized a government is, the less power women have in the public sphere.

3. Obeying Godde always takes precedence over cultural norms and mores.

Bible Study Helps

HERE ARE A LIST of books that can help you get on your way to studying the Bible. I've given two sets of Bible dictionaries and commentaries. For the more conservative readers who have a more literal view of how the Bible should be read, you'll want to look at the dictionaries and resources from InterVarsity Press. On the other hand, if you're more liberal and don't believe the Bible needs to be interpreted literally, you'll want to check out the resources from HarperCollins Publishers. The same goes with the two women's commentaries I've listed: the one edited by Katherine Clark Kroeger and Mary J. Evans is for the more conservative, and the commentary edited by Carol A. Newsome and Sharon H. Ringe is more liberal. All of these resources believe in the full equality of women.

Forth, Sarah S. *Eve's Bible: A Woman's Guide to the Old Testament*. New York: St. Martins Griffin, 2008.

Frymer-Kensky, Tikva. *Reading the Women of the Bible: A New Interpretation of Their Stories*. New York: Schocken Books, 2002.

Keener, Craig. *The IVP Bible Background Commentary: New Testament*. Downer's Grove: InterVarsity Press, 1993.

Kroeger, Catharine Clark and Richard Clark Kroeger. *I Suffer Not a Woman: Rethinking 1 Timothy 2:11–15 in Light of Ancient Evidence*. Grand Rapids: Baker Book House, 1992.

Kroeger, Catherine Clark and Mary J. Evans. *The IVP Women's Bible Commentary*. Downer's Grove: InterVarsity Press, 2002.

Mays, James L., ed. *HarperCollins Bible Commentary*. Revised edition. New York: HarperCollins, 2000.

Meyers, Carol, ed. *Women in Scripture: A Dictionary of Named and Unnamed Women in the Hebrew Bible, the Apocryphal/ Deuterocanonical Books, and the New Testament*. Grand Rapids: William B. Eerdmanns Publishing Company, 2000.

Newsome, Carol A. and Sharon H. Ringe, eds. *Women's Bible Commentary. Expanded edition*. Louisville: Westminster John Knox Press, 1998.

Powell, Mark Allan. *HarperCollins Bible Dictionary*. New York: HarperCollins Publishers, 2011.

Pritchard, James B. *HarperCollins Concise Atlas of the Bible*. New York: HarperCollins Publishers, 1997.

Vamosh, Miriam Feinberg. *Women at the Time of the Bible*. Nashville: Abingdon Press, 2008.

Walton, John H., Victor H. Matthews and Mark W. Chavalas. *The IVP Bible Background Commentary: Old Testament*. Downer's Grove, InterVarsity Press, 2000.

Works Cited

Camp, Claudia. "1 and 2 Kings." In *Women's Bible Commentary. Expanded edition*. Edited by Carol A. Newsome and Sharon H. Ringe. Louisville: Westminster John Knox Press, 1998.

Frymer-Kensky, Tikva. *Reading the Women of the Bible: A New Interpretation of Their Stories*. New York: Schocken Books, 2002.

John Chrysostom, "First Homily on the Greeting to Priscilla and Aquila," trans. by Catherine Clark Kroeger, Priscilla Papers 5.3 (Summer 1991), 18.

Kroeger, Catharine Clark, and Richard Clark Kroeger. *I Suffer Not a Woman: Rethinking 1 Timothy 2:11–15 in Light of Ancient Evidence*. Grand Rapids: Baker Book House, 1992.

Meyer, Marvin. *The Nag Hammadi Scriptures*. San Francisco: HarperCollins Publishers, 2007.

About Shawna R. B. Atteberry

Shawna R. B. Atteberry is an author, theologian, and storyteller. She writes biblical and feminist theology and urban fantasy. She also speaks at churches and conferences as well as preaches. Shawna has 15 years of experience in both writing and editing, and she is an ordained minister. She has 15 years of experience as a pastor holding various associate positions and as a laypastor. Her specialties are Biblical Studies, Feminist Theology, Spiritual Formation, and Christian Formation and Education. Shawna holds an M. A. Theological Studies and has been writing on the women in the Bible and women in church history for the last 15 years.

Shawna lives in Chicago with her husband Tracy and their cat Victoria. When she's not writing and speaking, she likes to read, have friends over, watch movies, crochet, and cook.

Scripture Index

www.ingramcontent.com/pod-product-compliance
Lightning Source LLC
Chambersburg PA
CBHW060419090426
42734CB00011B/2374

* 9 7 8 1 6 2 0 3 2 6 1 1 4 *